Alkal

Alkaline Diet For Beginners

The Ultimate Alkaline Diet
Guide With Over 60 Recipes

Andrew Kelvin

Your Free Gift

As a way of thanking you for the purchase, I'd like to offer you a complimentary gift:

- **5 Pillar Life Transformation Checklist:** This short book is about life transformation, presented in bit size pieces for easy implementation. I believe that without such a checklist, you are likely to have a hard time implementing anything in this book and any other thing you set out to do religiously and sticking to it for the long haul. It doesn't matter whether your goals relate to weight loss, relationships, personal finance, investing, personal development, improving communication in your family, your overall health, finances, improving your sex life, resolving issues in your relationship, fighting PMS successfully, investing, running a successful business, traveling etc. With a checklist like this one, you can bet that anything you do will seem a lot easier to implement until the end. Therefore, even if you don't continue reading this book, at least read the one thing that will help you in every other aspect of your life. Grab your copy now by clicking/tapping here or simply enter http://bit.ly/2fantonfreebie into your browser. Your life will never be the same again (if you implement what's in this book), I promise.

PS: I'd like your feedback. If you are happy with this book, please leave a review on Amazon.

Introduction

<u>Have you considered the possibility that your approach to losing weight, staying healthy and reversing as well as preventing development of disease has been all wrong?</u>

If you haven't, perhaps you should start thinking about it now.

Yes, you may have checked all the right boxes as far as conventional ways of eating healthy are concerned yet you still can't lose weight and keep it off or keep various diseases at bay. What could be the problem?

While you may have different theories as to why you are experiencing the problems you are going through, your acid alkaline balance (or imbalance) may be the simplest and most straightforward explanation for your problem.

If you are wondering how your acid alkaline balance relates to weight loss/weight gain and various diseases, this book will break everything down for you in an easy to follow language until you 'get it'. In addition to that, it will provide delicious recipes to hold you by the hand throughout the journey to attaining an optimal acid alkaline balance.

<u>To be more specific, you will learn:</u>

- The *<u>connection between health and the acid alkaline balance</u>*

- **The <u>concept of pH balance within your body system and how this relates to your weight and health</u>**

- How an alkaline diet <u>provides the needed balance for optimal health living, including weight loss</u>

- **Guidelines on what foods you can eat while on an alkaline diet and which foods you should avoid**

- How to <u>translate the allowed foods list to over 60 delicious breakfast, lunch, dinner, snacks, appetizers and, drinks recipes</u> to attain optimal health and lose weight

- **And much more!**

It doesn't matter whether you are following the conventional alkaline diet or the stricter version of it by Dr. Sebi; you will find this book very helpful. In fact, it is a stepping stone to Dr. Sebi's Electric Cell alkaline diet protocol.

Get started today to unlock secrets on how something as simple as your pH level could be the reason behind your life's struggles!

Table of Contents

Chapter 1: Understanding The Alkaline Diet

In the most basic form, the alkaline diet is a diet where you increase your intake of alkaline foods while reducing your intake of acidic-forming foods. The concept of the diet is that various types of food can affect the pH balance of your body.

The Fire Hypothesis

To explain further, your metabolism (process of converting food into energy) is occasionally compared to fire since each involves a chemical reaction where solid mass is broken down. The only difference is that the reactions in your body occur in a controlled and gradual manner.

When there is a fire there is a residue left behind in form of ash. Likewise, during the breaking down of food, an 'ash' residue is left behind in form of metabolic waste. This waste can be either acidic or alkaline.

It is believed that metabolic waste can actually affect your body's pH. That is, if you eat foods that leave behind an acidic ash once broken down, your acidic metabolic waste will make your blood more acidic and an alkaline ash will make your blood more alkaline. The acid ash hypothesis is of the thought that an acidic ash makes you more susceptible to diseases and illnesses, while a more alkaline one is seen as safeguarding.

Understanding pH

So what do I mean by alkaline and acidic? PH determines whether a component is acidic or alkaline and it ranges from 0 – 14 (from basic Chemistry you probably know this already):

Acidic is **0.0- 6.9**

Neutral is **7**

Alkaline is **7.1- 14.0**

The easiest way to monitor acidity/alkalinity is through measuring pH of the urine to ensure it stays over 7. However, is important to note that there is no set level of pH for all parts of the body and it varies considerably; some parts are acidic while other parts are alkaline. For instance, your stomach contains huge amounts of HCl (hydrochloric acid) which gives a highly acidic pH of 2-3.5 and this acidity is necessary to be able to break down food. Therefore, always remember that not all parts of the body require to be alkaline.

Why The Alkaline Diet?

First things first, it is important to understand how acidic-forming foods negatively affect our bodies; which is mainly through the red blood cells. The red blood cells have a mechanism that enables them to stay away from each other. This is basically a negative charge that keeps them separate from one another. Increased acidity in the blood can mess up this mechanism through robbing the red blood cells of the negative charge. This will lead to the red blood cells clumping up together, which will limit the levels of oxygen that enters your cells. Increased acidity in your blood; therefore, can lead to the weakening and death of red blood cells.

Now for the benefits of an alkaline diet:

Battles Fatigue

As explained earlier, too much acidity in your system decreases oxygen supply, which in turn decreases your cells' ability to repair and gather up nutrients. When your body lacks enough nutrients to give it energy, you will certainly feel weak. If you have been feeling tired and dazed through the day yet you had enough sleep, then you might need to check up on your acidity levels.

Boosts the immune system

An unbalance in pH lowers your body's ability to fight viruses and bacteria. Where there is lack of oxygen in the system (which acidity causes as explained above), viruses and bacteria flourish easily in the bloodstream. To eliminate the probability of diseases happening, alkalizing is essential.

Strengthens your bones

The more people age, the more the body uses up calcium especially, if you eat more acid based foods. This is because when we eat foods with high acidity, the body needs to balance the acid by dispensing calcium, magnesium and phosphorus. More than often, these minerals are taken from the bone stores, which can be a huge problem in the long run. But don't worry, with the alkaline diet, since you are not taking less of acid-forming foods, your body does not need to extract these minerals from your bones. In addition, you consume more of these minerals from the many alkaline foods high in these minerals

Healthier body and weight loss

The alkaline diet provides a base for a rather healthy diet. First, the diet requires you to cut out/reduce alcohol, red meats, sugars, trans fats and processed foods, which will definitely help you with weight loss and offer you other numerous health benefits. Also, the diet requires you to increase your intake of fresh and healthy foods such as veggies and fruits and water, which boost your general health and increase your chances of losing weight.

Alkaline Diet Guidelines

With that basic understanding of the alkaline diet, let us now learn what you can eat:

Fruits

Below are some of the fruits you can eat:

Lemon

Fresh Coconut

Grapefruit

Tomato

Cantaloupe

Bananas – the smallest one/ Burro/Manzana medium-size (original banana)

Berries – all varieties- Elderberries in any form – except cranberries

Figs

Pomegranate

Avocado

Currants

Cherries

Raisins

Papayas

Oranges

Grapes

Limes (key limes)

Melons

Sugar apples (cherimoya)

Pears

Dates

Soft Jelly Coconuts/ fresh coconut

Peaches

Apples (including crabapple)

Plums

Soursops –Latin or West Indian markets)

Prunes

Mango

Sprouts

Alfalfa Sprouts

Quinoa Sprouts

Kamut Sprouts

Mung Bean Sprouts

Amaranth Sprouts

Spelt Sprouts

Radish Sprouts

Soy Sprouts

Broccoli Sprouts

Fenugreek Sprouts

Vegetables

Chayote (Mexican Squash)

Bell Peppers

Cucumber

Garbanzo beans (chick peas)

Dandelion greens

Green Banana/Plantain

Lettuce

Mushrooms (all except Shitake)

Poke salad –greens

Tomato – (cherry, plum, and heirloom varieties only)

Purslane

Sea Vegetables

Squash (heirloom varieties)

Okra

Onions (chives, leeks, green onion)

Amaranth greens

Olives

Tomatillo

Turnip greens

Broad Beans

Beetroot

Broccoli

Cabbage

Carrot

Celery

Chard

Capsicum/Pepper

Cauliflower

Asparagus

Chives

Eggplant/Aubergine

Coriander

Cucumber

Courgette/Zucchini

Garlic

Collards

Green Beans

Endive

Radish

Dandelion

Kale

Kelp

Runner Beans

Onion

Peas

Snow peas

Pumpkin

Parsley

Spinach

Watercress

String Beans

Squashes

Wakame

Sweet Potato

Grains

It is not surprising that a majority of people nowadays have 'wheat allergies' and plenty of other 'gut' and stomach issues. This is mainly because wheat, together with a couple of other grains that we eat is not natural grains but hybrids of the originals generated by science. This renders them acidic whereas grains that grow naturally are alkaline based. Therefore, it is advisable that you eat the following grains instead:

Millet

Buckwheat

Spelt

Amaranth

Kamut

Rye

Teff

Fonio

Quinoa

Wild Rice/ BlackRice

Spices and Seasonings

Basil

Oregano

Marjoram

Achiote

Thyme

Dill

Sage

Ginger

Cayenne

Rosemary

Cilantro

Tarragon

Onion Powder

Bay leaf

Mint

Grasses

Wheatgrass

Barley Grass

Oat Grass

Shave Grass

Kamut Grass

Salty Flavors

Pure Sea Salt

(Kelp/Dulce/Nori– has "sea taste")

Powdered Granulated Seaweed

Pink Himalayan Rock Salt

Celtic Salt

Oils

Grape seed Oil (frying, deep-frying)

Avocado Oil (best for frying)

Walnut oil

Hemp oil (sautéing and for dressings)

Sesame oil

Extra Virgin Olive Oil (for cooking, sauté)

Cold Pressed Coconut Oil (for cooking, sauté, baking or butter substitute)

Flax oil

Seeds, Nuts, Nut Butters and Milk

Almonds

Hazelnut

Chia seed

Sunflower

Pumpkin

Hemp seed

Sunflower Seeds

Walnut

Tahini/sesame seed

Brazil Nut

Flax Seeds

Pine nuts

Coconut (yes it's a seed and nut)

Sesame Seeds

The following section includes foods that are not recommended for regular or general consumption if you are dealing with chronic health issues. It is for those on an alkaline diet and want to consume 'wholesome foods'.

Alkaline Processed Foods

If you have trusted sources of the following products (processed) you can purchase them; otherwise homemade is best. Well from that, you can enjoy the following products in:

Homemade Hummus

Homemade Spelt tortillas

Homemade Spelt Bread

Homemade Nut Cheese

Quinoa Pasta

Spelt Pasta

Kamut Pasta

Vitamins and Supplements

If you are taking any supplement or vitamins, it is very essential that it is from a plant based source. This is important because you find that many people have mineral deficiencies, even when taking supplements, because once you consume an oxide version or a synthetic mineral, your body only absorbs a miniscule of the mineral and the rest is processed as acidic waste. Plants however provide minerals that easily turn to liquid hence be absorbed fully through the body.

Acidic Foods to Avoid

The following should not be consumed or if you eat them, once in a while:

Animal Products (all)

Dairy products (all)

Sugar

Sweetened beverages

Processed foods

Wheat (another heavily grown GMO crop, and a hybrid of the original grains listed above)

Oats

Chapter 3: Alkaline Breakfast Recipes

Banana Muffins

Servings: 6

Ingredients

½ teaspoon salt

1 tablespoon vanilla extract

3 tablespoons ground flax seeds and 6-9 tablespoons water (egg substitute)

3 very ripe bananas, mashed

¼ cup oil

2 cups almond flour

1 tablespoon raw honey

1 teaspoon baking soda

Directions

Preheat your oven to 350 degrees F, and mix the flaxseed, honey, banana, vanilla and oil.

In a different bowl, mix the baking soda, almond flour and salt.

Gently add the dry ingredients into the banana mixture.

Spoon the batter into a greased muffin tin and bake for about 15 minutes. Insert a toothpick to check if it is done.

Flourless Banana Bread Muffins

Serves 9

Ingredients

3/4 cup almond flour/meal

2 tablespoons raw honey

1 teaspoon vanilla extract

1 tablespoon flaxseed plus 2 tablespoons water (combined)

½ cup rolled oats

½ teaspoon ground cinnamon

2 ripe medium bananas (200 g or a cup mashed)

2 tablespoons ground flaxseed

¼ cup almond butter

½ teaspoon baking soda

Directions

Preheat your oven to 375 degrees F and spray 9 cavities of your muffin tin with cooking spray. Place aside.

Toss all ingredients into your blender and run on high until the oats are broken down and the batter turns creamy and smooth.

Pour the batter into the muffin tins; fill them about 3/4 full.

Bake for about 10 to 12 minutes until the top of the muffins is set. Insert toothpick to check for doneness.

Let the muffins cool approximately for 10 minutes before you remove them. The muffins can keep in an airtight container for 10 days.

Recipe notes

You can substitute the almond butter for any other seed/ nut butter.

Super Seed Spelt Pancakes

Serves 3

Ingredients

42g flax seeds

½ teaspoon stevia extract

37.5g sesame seeds

¼ teaspoon fine sea salt

80g chia seeds

164g buckwheat groats

1 ½ teaspoons ground cinnamon

½ teaspoon baking powder

30g pumpkin seeds

2 tablespoons almond milk

1 teaspoon coconut oil

1 teaspoon baking soda

Directions

Grind the pumpkin seeds, sesame seeds, flax seeds, chia seeds and buckwheat groats into flour and keep ¼ of the seed flour for later use (not for this recipe).

Add 2 cups of the seed flour to a medium bowl.

Add in the rest of the ingredients but not the coconut oil. Pour in more milk if needed to attain the right consistency.

Add coconut oil to a non-stick pan and place over heat.

Once heated, pour thin layers of the batter and flip once you see bubbles form on top.

Cook until all the batter is used up.

Scrambled Tofu

Serves 1

Ingredients

3 cloves

1 onion

1/2 teaspoon of turmeric

Salt for taste

50g firm tofu

1/2 teaspoon of paprika

1 handful baby spinach

3 tomatoes

1/2 cup of yeast

1/2 teaspoon of cumin

Directions

Mince the garlic and dice up the onion.

Toss the onions into a pan and let them cook over medium heat for about 7 minutes. Add in the garlic and cook for 1 minute.

Toss in the tofu and tomatoes and cook for 10 more minutes. Add in some water, cumin and paprika and stir well. Continue cooking.

When the dish is about to cook, add in spinach, stir and once wilted, turn off the heat and serve.

Sprouted Buckwheat Crepes

Serves 4

Ingredients

1 tablespoon pure 100% vanilla extract

¾ cup pure water

1 cup buckwheat groats- soaked overnight

1 tablespoon chia seeds

Directions

Rinse buckwheat thoroughly and soak it in 1:2 parts water overnight.

Rinse then drain well the following morning.

Add all your ingredients to a blender and process until smooth.

Add coconut oil to a nonstick pan over high medium heat and pour in a thin layer to the center of your pan. Swirl the pan to make sure the batter spreads out- the texture should be thick enough to hold the shape for flipping.

Once the top is not liquid, flip and cook the other side until browned.

Do this with the rest of the batter.

Serve with some sprouted nut butter, fresh lemon juice, hemp seeds or whatever you like.

Breakfast Salad

Serves 2

Ingredients

1/2 pack of firm tofu

½ a red onion

2 spelt tortillas

1 avocado

4 handfuls of baby spinach

1 handful of almonds

2 tomatoes

1 pink grapefruit

1/2 lemon

Directions

Heat up the tortillas in an oven and once warm, bake for 8 to 10 minutes in the oven.

Chop up the onions, tomatoes and tofu and combine this. Put in the fridge and let it cool.

Now chop up the almonds, avocado and grapefruit. Mix everything well and place nicely around the bowl you had put in the fridge.

Squeeze a lemon on top all over the salad and enjoy!

Scrambled Tofu and Tomato

Serves 2

Ingredients

1 tablespoon coconut oil

A little coriander/cilantro

285g regular firm tofu

2 big handfuls of baby spinach

1/2 brown onion (or red if you fancy)

1 handful of arugula/rocket

Freshly ground black pepper

2 tomatoes

Himalayan/Sea salt

Pinch of turmeric

A little basil

½ small red pepper

A pinch of cayenne pepper

Directions

Use your hands to scramble the tofu into a bowl then chop and fry the onion quickly in a pan. Dice the peppers and do the same thing.

Dice the tomatoes and throw them into the pan. Toss in a pinch of turmeric, and add the spinach. Add salt and grind in the pepper. Cook until the tofu is warm and cooked.

Throw in basil leaves, coriander, the rocket just when the meal is about to be done. Serve with a pinch of some hot cayenne pepper.

You can serve on some toasted sprouted bread and some baby spinach.

Breakfast Patties

Serves 6

Ingredients

1 teaspoon sage

1/2 cup of garbanzo bean flour

1/2 teaspoon rosemary

1/2 teaspoon sea salt

1/2 teaspoon thyme

1/2 cup of spelt flour

1/2 teaspoon crushed red pepper

1 pinch ground clove

1/2 cup of spring water

1 pinch cayenne

1 tablespoon grapeseed oil

Directions

Add all ingredients into a medium sized bowl and mix to form a paste.

Place a skillet over medium high heat and drizzle some grapeseed oil into it.

Pour some batter into the skillet, cook for 3 minutes, flip and cook until ready.

Do this until all the batter is finished.

Sweet Potato Bombs

Serves 2

Ingredients

1 teaspoon ground flax seed

1 tablespoon chopped walnuts

1 tablespoon dried cherries

1 medium sweet potato, baked

1 tablespoon pumpkin seeds

1 teaspoon chia seeds

2 tablespoons organic, raw almond butter (smooth or chunky)

Directions

Start by baking your sweet potato. You can bake either in an oven or in the microwave. For the microwave, use a fork to prick the skin all over and place on a paper towel. Microwave for 3 to 4 minutes then place on foil and wrap for 3 to 4 minutes.

For the oven, also prick the skin using a fork and bake for 35 to 45 minutes at 425 degrees. Check for doneness by inserting a fork inside the potato.

Cut the cooked potato and use a fork to mash it up a bit. Spread the butter all over the potato and sprinkle some flax, walnuts, chia seeds and pumpkin seeds all over the potato.

Top with some dried cherries.

Enjoy!

Apple Quinoa Breakfast

Serves 2

Ingredients

1 1/2 cups water

1/2 cup quinoa

2 teaspoons cinnamon

2 large apples

Directions

Skin and core the apples and cut them into bite-sized pieces.

Add some water together with the apples and quinoa to a saucepan and bring to a boil. Cover and simmer for 20 to 25 minutes until the quinoa has absorbed the water and the apples are soft.

Add cinnamon and stir then pour into 2 separate bowls.

Drizzle some honey on top and add in more cinnamon if desired.

Amaranth Breakfast Porridge

Serves 6

Ingredients

1 cup amaranth

1 tablespoon ground cinnamon

2 cups water

4 tablespoons almond butter

2 cups almond milk

1/2 cup raw honey

Directions

Add the milk and water to a medium saucepan and bring to a boil. Add in the amaranth and whisk it in. Lower the heat to low and cover with the lid.

Simmer for about 30 minutes as you stir regularly until the amaranth is tender and the liquid is absorbed.

Remove from the heat, add in the cinnamon and drizzle some honey.

Serve while warm.

Alkaline Chocolate Chia Pudding

Serves 1

Ingredients

1 1/4 cups coconut milk

1 teaspoon vanilla extract

1 heaped tablespoon natural cacao powder

1/4 teaspoon Stevia extract

1/8 teaspoon ground cinnamon

1/8 teaspoon sea salt

¼ cup chia seeds

Directions

Add all ingredients to a mixing bowl and ensure everything is combined nicely. Add the pudding to a mason jar and let it rest overnight.

Stir nicely the next morning and dig in!

Chapter 4: Alkaline Lunch Recipes

Lentil-Stuffed Potato Cakes

Servings: 4

Ingredients

For the Cakes:

Salt

1 bay leaf

10 medium gold potatoes

1 cup potato starch- add more for dusting

For the Stuffing:

Coconut oil for panfrying

Salt and freshly ground black pepper

1 medium onion, chopped

4-ounces mushrooms

2 tablespoons olive oil

3⁄4 cup dried green lentils (preferably French lentils)- cooked

Directions

Combine the 7 cups of water, potatoes and bay leaf in a large pot and boil until the potatoes are tender. Poke with a fork to ensure they are cooked.

Rinse the potatoes under cold water when done; the skins will peel off easily. Now mash the potatoes until smooth and add the potato starch, stir to make dough. Add more potato starch if the dough feels too sticky.

For the stuffing, add olive oil to a sauté pan and place over medium high heat. Add in onions and cook as you stir for 5 minutes. Add in the lentils together with pepper and salt (to taste) and cook for 2 minutes. Set aside.

To make the cakes, scoop about 3 tablespoons of the dough on your hand and press it into your palm. Add a spoonful of stuffing on top of the dough and fold it over to close it. Shape it into a round disk.

Now add coconut oil to a skillet and heat over medium heat. Cook the potato cakes on both sides until golden, roughly 4 minutes per side.

Sesame Ginger Cauliflower Rice

Serves 4

Ingredients

2 tablespoons wheat-free tamari plus more to taste

4 cups finely chopped mushrooms

1 large head cauliflower

2 tablespoons toasted sesame oil

2 tablespoons grapeseed oil

1/2 teaspoon Celtic sea salt- plus more to taste

6 green onions- finely chopped (white and green parts)

1 bunch cilantro- finely chopped (1/2 cup)

2 tablespoons minced fresh ginger

2 teaspoons fresh lime juice- plus more to taste

1 small green chile- ribbed, seeded, and minced

4 teaspoons minced garlic (4 cloves)

Directions

For the cauliflower rice, roughly cut the cauliflower into florets and get rid of the tough middle core.

Fit a food processor with an S blade and add the florets to pulse. Pulse for a few seconds until the florets achieve a rice like consistency. You should have 5 to 6 cups of rice in the end.

Heat oil in a deep skillet or wok over medium high heat and fry the ginger, green onions, chili, garlic and mushroom seasoned with ¼ teaspoon of salt for 5 minutes. Once combined well and soft, add in the tamari and cauliflower rice and cook for 5 more minutes until soft.

Add in remaining salt, cilantro, and lime juice and adjust the flavors as desired.

Serve and enjoy!

Spinach With Chickpeas And Lemon

Serves 2

Ingredients

3 tablespoons extra virgin olive oil

Sea salt to taste (i.e. Celtic Grey, Himalayan, or Redmond Real Salt)

1/2 container grape tomatoes

1 large can of chickpeas (rinse well)

1 large onion- thinly sliced

1 tablespoon grated ginger

1 large lemon- zested and freshly juiced

1 teaspoon crushed red pepper flakes

4 cloves garlic- minced

Directions

Pour the olive oil into a large skillet and add in onion. Cook for about 5 minutes until the onion starts to brown.

Add in the ginger, lemon zest, garlic, tomatoes and red pepper flakes and cook for 3 to 4 minutes.

Toss in the chickpeas (rinsed and drained) and cook for an additional 3 to 4 minutes. Now add the spinach in 2 batches and once it starts to wilt, season with some sea salt and lemon juice.

Cook for 2 minutes.

Serve!

Avocado Cucumber Sushi Rolls

Serves 1

Ingredients

1 English Cucumber

Guacamole

1 cup curly kale leaves- ribs removed

Pinch of cayenne pepper- plus more to taste

1/8 teaspoon sweet paprika- to garnish

1 tablespoon fresh lemon juice

1 large avocado, peeled and pitted

1/4 teaspoon ground cumin

1/4 teaspoon Celtic sea salt

Directions

For the cucumber, use a wide vegetable peeler or a mandolin at the 1/16 inch setting to slice the cucumber into long slices lengthways on one side until you reach the seeds and then the other side, do the same thing.

Throw away the green tiny outer layers and set aside the inner long slices.

Mash the avocado in a bowl, and stir in chopped kale leaves, salt, cayenne, lemon juice and cumin and combine well. Adjust the salt, cayenne, cumin and lemon juice as desired.

To arrange, spread a quarter of the mixture using a spoon on each strip of the cucumber and roll up gently until you have a finished round roll- you might need to use a tooth pick to secure.

Put the rolls end down on a plate and sprinkle some smoked paprika on top.

Serve right away!

Spaghetti Squash Patties

Serves 2

Ingredients

1 spaghetti squash

3 g fresh coriander

2 tablespoons sunflower oil

1 spring onion

4g grated ginger

30g finely chopped leeks

1 teaspoon coriander

1 teaspoon ground flaxseed

Dressing

Pinch of Himalayan salt

5 tablespoons water

1 lemon juice

3 tablespoons tahini

Directions

Preheat your oven to 350 degrees F. Cut the spaghetti squash into half, down through the center. Scoop out the seeds and sprinkle with oil. Place on a baking tray and bake in the oven for 40 minutes.

Once done, let it cool then scoop out the insides using a fork and place on a bowl.

Slice the leeks and spring onions thinly and add this to the squash together with grated ginger, ground flax seed, chopped coriander and ground coriander, put in the fridge to cool.

Meanwhile, prepare the dressing. Add all the dressing ingredients to a bowl and whisk well using a fork; keep on mixing it even if it looks like it is curdling (it will eventually form a creamy and smooth dressing). You can add in more tahini if it is too thin and if it too thick you can add in a splash of water.

Heat the remaining sunflower oil in a skillet and once hot, use your hands to make palm sized patties using the squash mixture and place carefully in the skillet. Cook for 2 minutes on each side until golden.

Serve with the tahini dressing and a green salad.

Enjoy!

Super Alkaline Salad

Serves 4 to 6

Ingredients

For the Salad:

1 cup baby broccoli

4 cups baby kale

½ cup raspberries

1 sliced avocado

1 cup cucumber sliced or spiralized

1 cup watermelon

½ cup toasted almonds

1 cup papaya

For the Dressing

½ cup olive oil

½ cup master tonic (recipe below)

¼ cup goji berries

4 dates

Pinch sea salt

Master Tonic

1 jalapeno pepper- chopped

Juice of 1 lemon

32 ounces organic apple cider vinegar

1/4 cup garlic- minced

1/4 cup fresh ginger- chopped

2 tablespoons horseradish- minced

2 knobs turmeric- chopped

1/4 cup onion- chopped

Directions

For the Salad:

Mix all the salad ingredients together except the almonds.

For the tonic:

Add all the tonic ingredients to the apple cider vinegar. Blend the ingredients to combine but not to liquefy. Allow the tonic to set for about 1 to 2 weeks as you shake occasionally.

Sieve out the ingredients and pour the left-over master tonic into a jar and cover.

Use this tonic in your salad dressing.

For the dressing:

Combine the olive oil, salt and tonic. Add the goji berries and dates to the blender and combine until smooth.

Drizzle your dressing on the salad and sprinkle toasted almonds on top.

Enjoy!

Recipe Notes

You can explore with different variations of the tonic and once the ingredients differ, then the waiting time also differs; adjust accordingly.

Asian Sesame Dressing and Noodles

Serves 2

Ingredients

For dressing:

½ teaspoon lemon, freshly squeezed

1 clove garlic- minced

½ teaspoon liquid coconut nectar

2 tablespoons sesame butter

2 teaspoons tamari (gluten-free)

For noodle salad:

Optional: Sliced red bell pepper and/or carrot

1 tablespoon raw sesame seeds (topping)

1 scallion, chopped

1 package kelp noodles or 1 zucchini

Directions

For the noodles, you can use Kelp Noodles (a bag) or a zucchini (use a vegetable peeler or a spiralizer to make the noodles).

Combine all the dressing ingredients in a mixing bowl and use a spoon to thoroughly mix.

Make your zucchini noodles or if you are using kelp noodles, add to warm water for 10 minutes to rinse packaging liquid so that they can soften and separate. Add the sesame dressing to noodles and scallions and mix well.

Garnish with sesame seeds and serve.

Kale Salad with Avocado and Tomato

Serves 1-2

Ingredients

1/2 teaspoon ground black pepper

2 ripe tomatoes

1 ripe medium avocado

1/2 teaspoon of paprika

1 clove garlic crushed or 1/2 teaspoon garlic powder

1 tablespoon coconut nectar

2 large handfuls kale

Juice of 1 lime

Directions

Thoroughly wash the tomatoes and kale and chop them to bite-sized pieces. Add this to a mixing bowl or a large glass bowl.

Peel the avocado and add it to the bowl. Squeeze the juice from the lime into the kale mixture and add in the rest of the ingredients. Massage the ingredients together.

Serve and eat right away.

Raw Green Veggie Soup

Serves 4

Ingredients

2 stalks celery- chopped

1 small zucchini- chopped

1/4 cup fresh parsley

1 small watermelon radish for garnish- diced small

2 cups raw spinach

1/2 cup fresh cilantro

1 avocado

1/8 cup raw onion- chopped

1/4 teaspoon sea salt to taste

Juice of 1/2 to 1 lemon

1/4 cup raw almonds- preferably soaked over-night and rinsed

1½ cups filtered water

1 small garlic clove

2 slices green pepper

Directions

Add all ingredients to a blender except the sea salt and run the blender to achieve the desired consistency and warmth if using a Vitamix. If using a regular blender, then you will probably have to pour mixture into a saucepan and warm gently (but not heat) over low heat.

Adjust the seasoning as desired and squeeze a lime onto the soup to brighten the flavors as you wish.

Garnish with radish and dig in!

Kale Caesar Salad

Serves 1

Ingredients

1 large bunch of curly Kale

1/2 teaspoon sea salt

2 garlic cloves

1/3 cup almond nuts, raw

1/2 teaspoon smoked paprika

1 ¼ cups filtered water

1/8 teaspoon chipotle powder or to your liking – it's spicy

1½ teaspoons rice malt syrup

1 cup sunflower seeds (save a few for a garnish if desired)

Directions

Wash and dry your kale leaves. Remove the center just until where it thins out. Tear the leaf into bite size pieces and add to a large bowl. Measure the rest of the ingredients and add to a blender.

Run the blender until everything is fully incorporated and smooth. Pour half of this mixture over the kale and use your hands or 2 spoons to coat the kale.

Add the rest of the mixture bit by bit ensuring that the leaves are coated nicely even through the curls and folds. Leave for about 10 minutes for the kale leaves to tenderize and plate your greens.

Sprinkle some sunflower seeds on top if desired.

Enjoy!

Alkaline Dinner Plate

Serves 2

Ingredients

For the Kale

2 tablespoons of agave

Sea salt

1/2 cup chopped red onions

1/2 cup chopped sweet yellow, red, orange peppers and green onions

1/4 of habanero pepper (if desired)

2 bundles Kale greens

For the Pasta

1/2 teaspoon of grape seed oil

1 teaspoon sea salt

1 cup chopped portabella mushrooms

1/4 cup chopped red and green peppers

1 box Kamut pasta

1/2 cup chopped yellow squash

¼ cup chopped green and red onions

For the Fried Oyster Mushrooms

Cayenne pepper

½ large king oyster mushroom

Avocado slices (optional)

Spelt flour

Onion powder

Sea salt

Directions

Wash the kale and chop it. Coat the bottom of a pan with grapeseed oil and fry the peppers and onions. Add in kale with 2 tablespoons of agave. Let the kale cook for about 30 minutes over medium heat as you stir occasionally.

Add water to a pot and bring to a boil. Add in ½ teaspoon of grapeseed oil and a teaspoon of sea salt. Add in the kamut pasta and let this cook.

Sauté the peppers, portabella mushrooms and onions in a separate saucepan. Add the cooked pasta into the pan with veggies, add in chopped yellow squash and mix.

Rinse the oyster mushrooms lightly and season with cayenne, sea salt and onion powder as desired. Coat with spelt flour and fry slightly in some grapeseed oil. Remove and put on some paper towels to absorb the oil.

Serve while hot or warm.

Swiss Chard Taco Wraps

Serves 6

Ingredients

For the cumin-lime sauce:

1/2 teaspoon fine grain sea salt

1 teaspoon ground cumin + more if you like the heat

1 tablespoon honey

1/4 cup extra virgin olive oil

3 tablespoons fresh lime juice (from 1 to 2 large limes)

1/8 teaspoon crushed red pepper flakes

1 teaspoon lime zest

2 scallions, minced - white and light green parts only

For the wraps:

1 tablespoon olive oil

2 cups fresh cilantro- finely chopped

12 Swiss chard leaves with the stems removed

3 cups cooked wild rice

1 small bell pepper- diced

1 small red onion, diced

2 cups cherry tomatoes - sliced in half

1 (15-ounce) can lentils - rinsed and drained

Optional extras:

Diced avocado

Favorite hot sauce

A few pickled jalapeño peppers

Directions

Combine all of the dressing ingredients in a mason jar and cover with lid. Shake the jar and ensuring the dressing is well combined. You can also use a food processor or an immersion blender to mix. Taste to adjust the seasonings where needed.

Add olive oil into a large skillet and heat over medium heat. Add in the lentils, pepper, red onion and tomatoes. Cook until just heated or for about 5 to 8 minutes.

Toss in the cooked rice and cilantro and toss with the dressing. Season with some salt and mix.

For the tacos, scoop a hearty portion of the veggie combination into each chard leaf and wrap it up like a burrito or hold like a corn tortilla.

Dressing keeps well in the refrigerator for up to a week.

Carrot Salad

Serves 4

Ingredients

For the salad:

4 medium carrots grated

2 tablespoons walnuts chopped

2 tablespoons unsweetened shredded coconut

2-3 tablespoons chopped parsley

2 tablespoons pecans chopped

2 tablespoons pumpkin seeds

For the dressing

1/4 teaspoon ground black pepper

1 teaspoon grated fresh gingerroot

1/4 teaspoon salt

1 teaspoon coconut nectar

1 tablespoon avocado oil

1/2 teaspoon Dijon mustard

1 tablespoon apple cider vinegar

Directions

Mix all the salad ingredients in a large mixing bowl and set aside.

Combine the apple cider vinegar, gingerroot, salt and pepper, avocado oil, mustard, and nectar and whisk using a fork until well combined, and emulsifies a bit.

Pour the dressing over the salad and toss to combine.

Garnish with some more pumpkin seeds, grated coconut, and chopped parsley, if desired.

Serve right away or place in the fridge for a while.

Enjoy!

Veggies with Pumpkin Dressing

Serves 2 to 3

Ingredients

1½ cups vegetable stock

2/3 cup zucchini- diced

1/2 cup celery- diced

1/2 cup diced potatoes

3 tablespoons lemon juice

1 spring onion- sliced

2/3 cup carrots- diced

2/3 cup broccoli- diced

2 middle sized tomatoes- cubed

For the pumpkin dressing:

2 tablespoons lemon juice

2/3 cup vegetable stock

1/2 cup pumpkin, cooked and cooled

Sea salt & pepper

1 tablespoon olive oil

1 teaspoon Dijon-Mustard

Directions

Bring the stock to a boil and cook the potato, celery and carrots for about 8 minutes until firm to the bite. Reserve stock and set aside.

Add lemon juice to the cooked veggies and set aside.

Steam the zucchini and broccoli over hot water in a sieve for 5 minutes. Add all the vegetables including the spring onion and tomato in a large bowl and combine well with half of the reserved stock (or even less!).

Prepare the pumpkin dressing with the rest of the stock. Blend the pumpkin, lemon juice, oil, stock and mustard to form a paste and season with some pepper and salt.

Mix everything in a bowl, serve and enjoy.

Alkaline Super Salad

Serves 5

Salad

1/4 cup dry-roasted- unsalted walnuts

1 bunch of kale- cut into strips

1 grapefruit- sectioned

1 cup cucumber- cut into small strips

1/2 cup carrots- grated

1 small beet- grated

1/2 cup red cabbage- grated

Dressing

1/8 teaspoon ginger

2 shakes of cayenne

2 tablespoons tahini

1/4 teaspoon cinnamon

2 tablespoons cold-pressed extra virgin olive oil

2 tablespoons fresh lemon juice

Directions

Whisk together the dressing ingredients in a large bowl and add in kale to massage the dressing into the leaves to soften.

Toss in the rest of the ingredients and combine.

Enjoy!

Recipe notes

The recipe tastes better as the days go by because of the softening of the kale. Keep for up to 5 days in the fridge.

Sesame Noodle Bowl

Serves 2

Ingredients

8 ounces spelt angel hair pasta

For the dressing:

1 cucumber- peeled and finely chopped (about 2-3 cups)

Freshly squeezed juice of 1 lime (about 1 tablespoon)

2 tablespoons rice vinegar

2 tablespoons toasted sesame oil

2 teaspoons minced fresh garlic

3 tablespoons tamari

2 teaspoons chili garlic sauce (available in good grocery stores)

1 tablespoon tahini

1 tablespoon creamy almond butter

1 tablespoon freshly grated ginger

For the garnish:

Lime wedges

½ cup fresh cilantro

1 bunch sliced scallions

Black sesame seeds

Directions

Cook the pasta in accordance to the package instructions. Drain in a colander and run cold water to cool. Let the pasta drain in the colander and stir occasionally until completely dry.

Add all dressing ingredients into a large bowl and combine well until the almond butter and tahini incorporate smoothly. Add in pasta and mix gently to coat (tongs work best here).

Pour into a plate and garnish each with a lime wedge, scallions, cilantro and black sesame seeds.

Carrot Apple Ginger Soup

Serves 4

Ingredients

Fine sea salt to taste

1 large apple

1 pound carrots

1 tablespoon freshly grated ginger root

1 tablespoon unsweetened and unflavored almond milk (or other plant milk of your choice)

½ cup raw cashews

4 cups low sodium vegetable broth

Directions

Place the cashews in water to soak for at least 8 hours. Drain and pour into a food processor together with the ginger root and almond milk.

Process until smooth and if too thick add some almond milk a little at a time. The mixture should be somehow pourable.

Peel and core your apple into small chunks. Peel and chop the carrots into 1-inch chunks. Mix the apples and carrots and steam for about 5 minutes until tender. Transfer to a large soup pot to slightly cool.

Pour in the veggie broth and use an immersion blender to blend until you can no longer feel any clumps. You can also use a blender or a food processor as long as you first let the soup reach room temperature.

Add soup to a large pot, add in the cashew-ginger mixture and stir to incorporate. Add 2 teaspoons of salt, stir, and taste to adjust accordingly. It should have a bright taste with a 'bite' of ginger flavor.

Heat the soup before serving but don't let it boil.

This soup can keep well in the fridge for up to 3 days- freezes well too.

Savory Avocado Wraps

Serves 1

Ingredients

½ tomato- diced

Green jalapeño pepper, to taste (optional)

1 teaspoon cilantro- chopped

½ Hass avocado- sliced

1 lettuce leaf (butter lettuce or romaine best)

Alfalfa sprouts (optional)

¼ red onion- diced, or to taste

Sea salt (Celtic Grey, Himalayan, or Redmond Real Salt) and pepper to taste

Small handful of spinach

½ teaspoon cumin

Directions

Spread the avocado on the lettuce leaf and sprinkle some red onion, cumin, pepper, diced tomato, cilantro and sea salt. Add spinach and fold in half.

Enjoy!

Chapter 5: Alkaline Dinner Recipes

Alkalizing Green Soup

Serves 2

Ingredients

1 tablespoon sunflower or coconut oil

1 pint of stock made with 1 tablespoon vegetable Bouillon powder

1/4 tablespoon fennel seeds

½ red onion- finely chopped

1 cup tender stem broccoli

1¼ cups baby spinach

Juice and zest of 1 lemon

1 clove garlic- finely chopped

Directions

Fry the garlic, red onions, and fennel seeds in oil over medium heat for about 2 minutes.

Add in the broccoli, zest, stock and lemon juice and let it cook for 4 minutes.

Remove from heat and toss in the baby spinach. Stir until the spinach is wilted.

Immediately add the mixture to a blender and blend until smooth.

Serve while hot.

Healing Ginger Carrot Soup

Serves 2

Ingredients

1 tablespoon fresh ginger

Sea salt and pepper- to taste

2 garlic cloves

½ onion- quartered

4 carrots- washed and peeled

2 cups vegetable stock

1 teaspoon turmeric

Directions

Add all your ingredients to a large pot and bring to a boil. Once boiled, let it simmer for an hour. When the carrots are soft, blend using an immersion blender until smooth.

Garnish with some hemp seeds on top if desired.

Enjoy!

Kale Salad

Serves 1-2

Ingredients

Salad

½ (or a whole) avocado

2 handfuls of sprouts (any kind)

1 head lacinato kale (also called dinosaur kale)

1 medium-to large tomato

Dressing

½ tablespoon olive oil (optional)

1 teaspoon Dijon mustard

4 drops liquid stevia

4 Tablespoons nutritional yeast

Juice of 1 lemon

Cayenne pepper to taste

Optional toppings:

Sunflower or pumpkin seeds

A few strips of seared tempeh

Regular tempeh

Directions

Discard the kale stems (can discard or keep for juicing later on) and use your hands to tear up the kale into bite sized pieces. Put the kale in a large bowl.

Sprinkle some salt and massage for a couple of minutes to help break down the kale.

Combine the dressing ingredients in a small bowl. Mix it into the kale by massaging (don't be afraid to get your hands dirty as this will help make the kale softer).

Cut the toppings and add to the salad bowl.

Toss and serve right away.

Avocado, Kale and Kelp Noodles Salad

Serves 2

Ingredients

1 carrot julienned or shredded

Sea salt and black pepper to taste

3 cups kale- stems removed and very thinly sliced

½ large avocado

¼ cup sauerkraut

6 ounces kelp noodles (2 cups or half the package)

Juice of half a lemon

Directions

Combine the carrots, kale, kelp noodles and sauerkraut with the lemon and add in the avocado. Use a fork to smash the avocado and then your hands to incorporate everything together.

Taste and adjust as desired, season with fresh pepper and dig in!

Recipe notes

You can substitute the kelp noodles for very thinly sliced 2 cups of cabbage- still delicious and super nutritious.

You can leave out the raw sauerkraut if you don't have any.

Alkaline Green Soup

Serves 2

Ingredients

200g zucchini, roughly sliced

½ teaspoon ground coriander

2 garlic cloves, sliced

1 thumb-sized piece ginger, sliced

3 teaspoons sunflower oil

1 pinch of pink Himalayan salt

1 small pack parsley, roughly chopped- reserve a few whole leaves to serve

85g broccoli

500ml stock- made by mixing 1 tablespoon of vegetable stock powder with some boiling water in a jug

100g kale, chopped

1 lime- zested and juiced

½ teaspoon ground turmeric

Directions

Add oil to a deep pan and fry the garlic, turmeric, ginger, coriander and salt over medium heat for about 2 minutes then pour in 3 tablespoons of water to add some moisture to the spices.

Add in the zucchini and mix well to ensure all slices are coated with the spices and cook for 3 more minutes. Add 400 ml veggie stock and allow to simmer for 3 minutes.

Add in lime juice, broccoli and kale and the rest of the stock and let this cook for 3 to 4 minutes until the veggies are tender.

Remove from the heat and add in chopped parsley. Pour this into a blender and blend until smooth (on high speed) to get a nice green soup with bits of dark specks through (the kale).

Garnish with some parsley and lime zest.

Enjoy your soup!

Simple Salad

Serves 2

Ingredients

2 tablespoons toasted pumpkin seeds

1 avocado sliced or chopped

1/4 cup cashews- optional

1 red onion thinly sliced optional

2 mandarin oranges separated into slices

2 tablespoons toasted sesame seeds

1 bag stir fry veggies organic is best

Dressing

1-2 tablespoons fresh cilantro chopped- to garnish

1 bottle Asian Dressing- make sure it is organic

Directions

Add the veggies to a bowl and toss with your dressing and cover. Let this rest for the flavors to incorporate.

To serve, toss the veggies again to ensure the salad is covered with dressing and serve over leafy greens. Top with some orange slices, pumpkin seeds, sesame seeds and slices of avocado. Garnish with chopped cilantro and enjoy!

Avocado Hemp Dinner Salad

Serves 1

Ingredients

1 head red leaf lettuce

Black Pepper- fresh ground

1 lemon

1 avocado

1 English cucumber

1 tomato

Pink Himilayan salt- to taste

Directions

Chop the avocado and combine with lemon juice.

Cut the rest of the ingredients and combine with the avocado lemon mixture.

Serve and enjoy!

Alkaline Watercress Salad

Serves 2

Ingredients

For the Salad:

1/2 cucumber- sliced

A few sprouts- such as clover or alfalfa

2 large handfuls parsley- chopped coarsely

1 cup watercress

1/2 avocado- in small cubes

For the Dressing:

1/2 avocado

1-2 teaspoons kelp powder

1/2 cucumber, in chunks

Juice of one large lemon or lime

¼ cup olive oil

Unprocessed salt and pepper to taste

1 small garlic (optional)

Directions

First, make the salad. Arrange all the salad ingredients in a large salad bowl nicely.

For the dressing, add all the dressing ingredients except the avocado into a blender or food processor and puree until creamy and smooth. Add in the avocado and puree again. Thin with a bit of filtered water if too thick, a tablespoon at a time. Add to a small bowl and serve aside the salad.

Enjoy!

Green Soup

Serves 4

Ingredients

2 ½ cups water

1 clove garlic

1 tablespoon nutritional yeast

1 tablespoon miso

1 ounce parsley leaves (a handful)

1 ounce cilantro leaves (a handful)

1 large celery stalk

2 tablespoons coconut cream*

2 ounces (2 handfuls) spinach- de-stemmed

1 cup cooked split green peas

Toppings: any or all of the following

Celery and/or cilantro leaves

Toasted almonds

Shaved watermelon radish (you can soak in salt water)

Directions

Mix together the spinach, parsley, garlic, nutritional yeast, water, split peas, celery, cilantro, miso and a tablespoon of the coconut cream. Puree until really smooth.

Add to a medium saucepan and heat gently to warm if desired (hot but not simmering). Taste and adjust the miso or salt as needed.

Serve and top with the rest of the cream and whatever toppings you chose to use.

Recipe notes

You can use the cream on the top of a can of full fat coconut milk.

Kale Pesto Pasta

Serves 2

Ingredients

2 cups fresh basil

Sea salt and pepper

1 zucchini, noodled (spiralizer)

1/2 cup walnuts

2 limes, fresh squeezed

1 bunch kale

1/4 cup extra virgin olive oil

Optional: garnish with sliced asparagus, tomato and spinach leaves

Directions

Soak the walnuts the previous night to make absorption easier.

To prepare the dressing, add the ingredients to a food processor or blender except the garnishes and zucchini noodles and puree to get desired consistency.

Plate the zucchini noodles, pour the dressing over, toss and serve.

Grilled Asparagus and Mushroom Tacos

Serves 4

Ingredients

Lime wedges

4 garlic cloves, crushed with press

1 cup homemade or prepared guacamole

1/2 teaspoon Kosher salt

Hot sauce- for serving

3 tablespoons canola oil

Cilantro sprigs

8 ounces mushrooms, stems discarded

1 bunch green onions, trimmed

1 teaspoon ground chipotle chile

Directions

Heat grill on medium setting. Combine the salt, chipotle, garlic and onion in a large baking sheet and add in the green onions, asparagus and mushrooms. Toss to coat the veggies well.

Grill asparagus until tender and charred a bit, ensuring that you turn often- about 4 to 5 minutes. Now place the veggies onto a chopping board.

Cut green onions and asparagus to 2-inch lengths and chop the mushrooms. Serve with some guacamole cilantro, lime wedges and hot sauce.

Alkaline Electric Vegetable Quinoa

Serves 6 to 8

Ingredients

1/4 cup yellow bell peppers- diced

2 teaspoons sea salt

1 teaspoon oregano

1/2 teaspoon cayenne powder

1 cup zucchini- chopped

1 roma / plum tomato- diced

1/4 cup green bell peppers- diced

4 cups cooked quinoa

1/4 cup red bell peppers- diced

1 tablespoon onion powder

2 tablespoon grape seed oil / olive oil (optional)

1/2 cup red onion- diced

1 teaspoon basil

1/2 cup spring water

Directions

Pour oil into a large skillet or pan and heat oil over medium high heat. Once the oil is hot, fry the seasonings and veggies for about 5 to 10 minutes.

Add water and quinoa and cook for 5 more minutes.

Serve and enjoy!

Alkaline Mushroom Salad

Serves 4

Ingredients

Romain Lettuce

1 mango

1 teaspoon Grape seed oil

1 cup chopped red/ yellow/ orange sweet mini peppers

Cilantro, avocado, sea salt, cayenne, hemp seed milk agave (salad dressing)

Portabella mushrooms

¼ cup red onions and green onions

1 organic squash

1 organic zucchini

1 cup strawberries

Directions

Fry the peppers, mushroom, and onions and diced squash in a pan with grapeseed oil over medium heat.

Wash and cut zucchini, fruit and lettuce and add to a salad bowl.

Add the homemade avocado dressing and sauté mushrooms.

Enjoy!

Chapter 6: Alkaline Snack and Appetizers

Raw Cacao, Pistachio & Almond Balls

Servings: 12

Ingredients

¼ cup almonds

4 Medjool dates (this means 1.3g of sugar per ball which is okay)

½ cup shredded coconut

1 tablespoon chia seeds

1/3 cup alkaline Dutch cacao powder

1/3 cup chestnuts

1/3 cup coconut oil

1 cup almond meal

Directions

Place the almonds and dates in hot water to soften; the almonds should be soaked for at least 4 hours and the dates about an hour after removing the seed (but if using a high-speed food processor or blender then skip this step).

Add the almond meal, half of the chestnuts, coconut oil, chia, dates, almonds, shredded coconut and cacao to your blender or processor and blend.

Add to a bowl and let this stand for a couple of minutes so that the chia can soften and expand.

Smash the rest of the chestnuts and roll the raw mixture into balls. Roll over the crushed nuts to coat.

This will keep in fridge for up to 7 days.

Almond Berry Cake

Servings 10

Ingredients

40g almonds for garnish

2 teaspoons vanilla extract

1 punnet blackberries to serve

1/2 cup water

3/4 cups vegan butter

3 1/3 cups ground almonds

1 teaspoon baking powder

1/2 cup slivered almonds to garnish

2 1/2 cups blackberries to serve

1 punnet raspberries

1/4 cup coconut sugar

Directions

Preheat your oven to 175 degrees C and use parchment paper to line a baking tray.

Add raspberries together with some water and vanilla extract to a pan and simmer gently for about 7 to 8 minutes over medium heat, using a whisk to mix until smooth. Set aside and let this cool.

Mix the coconut sugar and eggs in a different bowl and mix the almonds and butter together. Add in raspberry puree and baking powder to the mix.

Line a baking tray and pour the mixture in. Sprinkle some flaked almonds on top and bake in the oven for about 15 minutes.

Meanwhile, prepare the blackberries and a tin foil that is large enough to cover your cake.

Quickly remove the cake from the oven and add the blackberries on top the half-baked cake and use the tinfoil to cover it. Put back in the oven for about 20 minutes.

Once the 20 minutes are over, remove from the oven and insert a knife to check for doneness- if it comes out clean then it is done.

Place on a cooling rack and once cooled enjoy!

Sweet Potato Chips

Serves 4

Ingredients

Sea salt (Celtic Grey, Himalayan, or Redmond Real Salt) & black pepper to taste

4-5 sweet potatoes

Coconut oil

Optional: Cumin to taste

Directions

Preheat your oven to 200 degrees F.

Fit a mandolin with a thin slice blade and slice the sweet potato using it (this is better than a knife as the sweet potatoes will bake much better).

When you are done slicing the sweet potatoes, add them to a large bowl and drizzle some coconut oil on top. Season with some black pepper, salt and cumin (if using). Toss to combine and place the seasoned sweet potato slices on a baking sheet lined with parchment paper evenly.

Put this in a preheated oven and bake for about 45 minutes, flip over and bake for 45 more minutes to an hour until the slices look really toasted.

Let them cool on the baking sheet before you serve.

You can add more spices if desired.

Cauliflower 'Buffalo Wings' With Barbeque Sauce

Serves: 4

Ingredients

1/2 teaspoon of Himalayan salt

1 cup of water

1 teaspoon of garlic powder

1 cup of chickpea flour

1 head of cauliflower, chopped into bite-sized pieces

Barbeque sauce ingredients:

1 teaspoon ground coriander

1 teaspoon ground cumin

1/2 teaspoon cayenne pepper

1/3 cup (80ml) organic tomato sauce

1 teaspoon ground allspice

1 teaspoon lemon juice

1 tablespoon coconut oil

1 tablespoon Worcestershire sauce

1 tablespoon Dijon mustard

2 garlic cloves- crushed

1 small brown onion- grated

Directions

Preheat your oven to 450 degrees F.

Add the salt, water, garlic powder and flour to a bowl and whisk until you have a smooth batter.

Toss the above mixture with the cauliflower and bake in the preheated oven for 15 to 20 minutes making sure to mix them up half way through.

To make the barbeque sauce:

Add coconut oil to a pan and warm over low heat. Add in the cumin, allspice, garlic, coriander, cayenne and onion and cook as you stir for 4 to 5 minutes and then pour in the lemon juice.

After about a minute, add in the tomato sauce, Worcestershire sauce, 250 ml of water and mustard. Adjust the heat to medium and season your sauce with Himalayan salt and some black pepper when almost boiling. Lower heat and simmer for about 10 to 15 minutes.

When it is thickened, let this cool then blend until smooth.

Enjoy!

Beetroot Hummus

Serves 6

Ingredients

2 tablespoons tahini

1/2 teaspoon smoked paprika

Olive oil

3 small beets, about ½ pound

1/2 – 1 teaspoon sea salt

Juice of 1 lemon

1/4 teaspoon chile flakes

1 (15 ounce) can chickpeas, rinsed and drained

2 cloves garlic, chopped

Almonds and cilantro for topping

Directions

Preheat your oven to 425 degrees F.

Wash the beets over running tap water and put in an aluminum foil. Add a bit of olive oil and some salt and wrap the beets loosely inside the foil.

Roast in the oven for about 40 to 45 minutes. Let this cool then peel once cool enough to hold with your hands. Dice to cubes and set aside.

Place the diced beets, lemon juice, pressed garlic, paprika, chickpeas, tahini, sea salt and chile flakes to a blender or food processor. Blend until smooth and add in olive oil as need be until you get the desired consistency.

Serve in a bowl with your favorite spelt tortillas.

Enjoy!

Spicy Buffalo Cauliflower Popcorn

Serves 2

Ingredients

2 heads of cauliflower

Spicy Buffalo Sauce:

2 - 3 tablespoons nutritional yeast- optional

¾ -1 cup dates

2 teaspoons garlic powder

1-2 teaspoon cayenne pepper

½ teaspoon turmeric

2 teaspoons onion powder

2 tablespoons raw tahini

¼ cup sun-dried tomatoes

½ cup filtered water

Directions

Cut up cauliflower into small bits making sure the florets are as small as they can be to make your popcorn super crunchy and flavorful.

Toss all the buffalo sauce ingredients into a high-speed blender and blend to achieve a thick and uniform consistency.

Spoon or pour this mixture into a large mixing bowl and set aside.

Add the cauliflower florets into the spicy buffalo mixture and stir well until every floret is coated well on every side.

Place the coated florets on dehydrator trays. Sprinkle some sea salt and some herbs if using.

Dehydrate for about 12 to 24 hours at 155 degrees F until the desired crunchiness is achieved. The more time you give them, the crunchier they will be.

Recipe notes

Soak the sundried tomatoes in water about an hour ahead of preparing.

To store, place in an airtight container in the fridge for a couple of days.

If you can't use a dehydrator, bake in the oven at the lowest temperature possible.

Sesame Carrot Fries

Serves 4

Ingredients

1 teaspoon black or white sesame seeds

1 teaspoon toasted sesame oil

4 carrots- peeled- halved crosswise and cut into thin matchsticks

1 tablespoon olive oil or grapeseed oil

¼ teaspoon salt

Directions

Preheat your oven to 425 degrees F and use a large parchment paper to line a large rimmed baking sheet.

Add the carrots, sesame oil, sesame seeds and olive oil into a medium bowl and toss. Transfer to baking sheet and spread the mixture into a single layer.

Roast in preheated oven until the carrots begin caramelizing and turning crisp, about 25 to 30 minutes.

Remove from the oven, cool and enjoy!

Sweet Potato Toast with Almond Butter

Serves 6

Ingredients

1 large banana- peeled and thinly sliced

Fine salt

4 tablespoons almond butter

1 tablespoon coconut oil- melted

¼ cup toasted coconut chips

2 medium sweet potatoes (about 1 pound total)

Directions

Preheat your oven to 450 degrees F.

Slice the sweet potatoes on the 4 long sides of each sweet potato such that they can sit flat on the cutting board. Now slice the potatoes lengthwise into about half an inch thick planks that are 5 inches by 2 inches (you will get about 3 planks for each sweet potato).

Mix the sweet potatoes with a pinch of salt and some coconut oil in a mixing bowl and toss lightly to coat.

Spread out the coated potatoes on a baking sheet and roast in oven until they are lightly browned, about 15 minutes, ensuring that you flip when they are half way through- insert knife to check for doneness.

Remove the potatoes from the oven and transfer to plates. Divide the almond butter among each sweet potato piece and top with a slice of banana and sprinkle with some toasted coconut.

Serve right away!

Recipe notes

You can make the toasts as meal preps and store in the fridge in an airtight container for up to 4 days. To reheat, do it in a toaster until warm all through.

Homemade Almond Butter Cups

Serves 8

Ingredients

½ cup almond butter

½ cup coconut oil

¼ cup raw honey

¼ cup Dutch cacao powder

Directions

Add the almond butter, raw honey and coconut oil into a small saucepan and melt.

Add in the raw cocoa powder and whisk well to combine.

Spoon this mixture to mini muffin liners and put in the freezer until hardened. Keep them in freezer or refrigerator until when ready to serve.

Chapter 7: Alkaline Drinks

Alkaline Smoothie

Serves 2

Ingredients

1 cup ice

5 strawberries frozen

1 teaspoon chia seeds

1 cup watermelon cubed

1 handful fresh spinach

1 cup almond milk

1/2 small banana

Directions

Add all your ingredients to the blender. Run the blender until everything is smooth and creamy.

To prevent the smoothie from turning brown, combine the banana with the greens, chia seeds and half of the ice then half of the almond milk. Then blitz together the strawberries, watermelon, ice and almond milk.

Serve and enjoy.

Alkalizing Juice

Serves 1

Ingredients

1 apple (preferably green)

1 bunch celery

1 cucumber

Directions

Start by removing the core from the apple. Add everything to your juicer and voila!

You can also use a blender for this recipe and strain the pulp later on (or drink it as it is since it's a great source of fiber).

Alkaline Kiwi Green Smoothie

Serves 2

Ingredients

1/4 cup water

2 teaspoons pure honey

1 teaspoon lemon zest

1 cup spinach- tightly packed

Small handful fresh mint- about 10 large leaves

1 tablespoon raw coconut oil- optional

1/2 English cucumber- diced (skin on)

1 green apple- peeled and sliced

1 banana

Juice of 1/2 lemon- medium

1 kiwi- sliced in half and flesh spooned out

Directions

Add all your ingredients to a blender and blend for 30 to 60 seconds or until creamy and smooth. Add in an extra banana or some honey to adjust the sweetness.

Fennel and Mint Tea

Serves 1 to 2

Ingredients

2 cups alkaline water- boiled

¼ cup fresh mint leaves (can be also a tea bag)

Few inches of ginger- sliced

1 fennel tea bag

Directions

Boil your water and add ginger and boil for 5 more minutes. Remove from heat and set aside. Add in mint leaves and fennel tea bag.

Cover and let this rest for 10 minutes.

Drain and serve!

Coconut Water Lemonade

Serves 4 to 6

Ingredients

1/2 cup freshly squeezed lemon juice

2 cups ice

2 lemons sliced

67.6 ounces or 2 liters of coconut water

1 small bunch mint

Directions

Combine the lemon juice, and coconut water in a pitcher. Stir well to combine.

Add in the slices of lemon, ice and fresh mint into the jug.

Pour yourself some and enjoy.

Veggie Blast Smoothie

Serves 1-2

Ingredients

1/2 onion

1 cup of spinach or kale- juiced

Black pepper and Himalaya salt to taste

1 cucumber- peeled and sliced

1 lemon- juiced

1 tablespoon olive oil

4 tomatoes- peeled

1 garlic clove

Directions

Blend your veggies and mix with the lemon juice, pepper, salt and spinach juice.

Serve and enjoy!

Carrot Apple Ginger Juice

Serves 1

Ingredients

1/2 green apple cored

Pinch of Celtic sea salt

1 stalk celery (including leaves)

1 handful baby spinach (or kale)

1/2 English cucumber

1 (1/2-inch) piece fresh ginger root

1 lemon- rind removed

1 carrot- scrubbed

Directions

Push everything through a juicer and pour into a glass.

Beet, Lemon and Ginger Juice

Ingredients

1 1/2 inch piece of ginger

1 lemon peeled

4 medium beets peeled (having them peeled is best to avoid a strong dirt taste)

Directions

Peel your beets if you haven't yet. Add all your ingredients to your juicer.

Pour into a glass and serve right away.

Enjoy!

Good Ol' Lemonade

Serves 2

Ingredients

Mineralized water

Ice cubes

2 cups freshly squeezed lemon juice

Slices of lemon

Directions

Add water to a pitcher and pour in squeezed lemon juice.

Throw in your ice cubes and slices of lemon.

Blueberry Banana Smoothie

Serves 1

Ingredients

1/2 cup water

1/2 tablespoon hemp seeds- optional

1/2 cup ice

1 teaspoon alkaline greens powder

1/2 tablespoon ground flaxseed- optional

1 ripe banana

½ cup blueberries

1/2 cup almond milk

Directions

Add all your ingredients (reserving some hemp seeds and blueberries to garnish) to a blender and run until creamy and smooth for about 1 to 2 minutes.

Garnish with some hemp and blue berries if desired.

Enjoy!

Tropical Alkaline Breeze

Yields 24 ounces juice

Ingredients

Young Thai coconut juice

4½ cups carrots

1½ cups chopped Celery

Directions

Extract the juice from your coconut and push everything through your juicer.

Delicious Alkaline Green Milk

Serves 1 to 2

Ingredients

2 cups of spinach + a few inches of ginger, juiced

1 cup coconut milk

Pinch of cinnamon

Juice of 1 lemon

1 cup almond milk

Directions

Warm up the coconut and almond milk on low heat and cook for a couple of minutes. Add in cinnamon and combine well. Set aside.

Add in the ginger juice, lemon juice and fresh spinach juice.

Serve while warm.

Enjoy!

Blueberry Banana Smoothie

Serves 2

Ingredients

1 cup unsweetened almond milk

½ cup blueberries preferably

1 ripe banana

2-3 tablespoons almond butter- preferably sprouted or soaked

1 teaspoon vanilla extract

Directions

Combine all the ingredients in a quart size and wide mouth mason jar. Use a handheld blender to blend until smooth.

Serve right away and store the leftovers in the refrigerator.

Lime Alkaline Smoothie

Serves 2

Ingredients

1/2 English cucumber, roughly chopped

2 medium limes, peeled and halved

2 cups firmly packed baby spinach

¾ cup raw coconut water (or filtered water)

1 medium avocado, peeled and pitted

2 cups ice cubes

1 teaspoon finely grated lime zest

20 drops liquid stevia plus more to taste

Pinch of Celtic sea salt

Directions

Add everything into a blender and run the blender for 30 to 60 seconds on high until everything is fully combined, smooth and creamy.

Adjust the sweetener as need be.

Gazpacho

Serves 2

Ingredients

4 large beefsteak tomatoes

¼ cup fresh cilantro

2 large cloves garlic

1 teaspoon sea salt

1 cucumber

3 tablespoons extra virgin olive oil

1 red bell pepper

¼ cup fresh parsley

½ freshly squeezed lime

½ red onion

1 teaspoon black pepper

1 freshly squeezed lemon

Directions

Add everything to a blender and blend. Leave the cold soup slightly chunky or even smooth (whichever way you prefer it).

Enjoy!

Conclusion

We have come to the end of the book. Thank you for reading and congratulations for reading until the end.

I truly hope you found the book extremely helpful and actionable in moving to the next level of living a healthy life where weight is not part of your struggles!

If you found the book helpful, would you mind posting a review of the book on Amazon? It would be highly appreciated!

Do You Like My Book & Approach To Publishing?

If you like my writing and style and would love the ease of learning literally everything you can get your hands on from Fantonpublishers.com, I'd really need you to do me either of the following favors.

1: First, I'd Love It If You Leave a Review of This Book on Amazon.

2: Check Out Books

Visit my author profile on Amazon to check the latest books I have on the alkaline diet and its stricter version by Dr. Sebi. I believe you will find my alkaline diet books very helpful.

To get a list of all my other books, let me send you the list by requesting them below: http://bit.ly/2fantonpubnewbooks

3: Grab Some Freebies On Your Way Out; Giving Is Receiving, Right?

I gave you a complimentary book at the start of the book. If you are still interested, grab it here.

5 Pillar Life Transformation Checklist: http://bit.ly/2fantonfreebie

38380813R00081